Glad to wear Glasses

(GLAD TO HAVE EARS)

Glad to wear Glasses

John Hegley

with illustrations by
Linda Leatherbarrow and
John Hegley

André Deutsch

First published in November 1990 by
André Deutsch Limited
105-106 Great Russell Street
London WC1B 3LJ
Second impression November 1990
Third impression December 1990
Fourth impression July 1991
Fifth impression January 1992
Sixth impression June 1992
Seventh impression January 1993
Eighth impression March 1993
Ninth impression January 1994

ISBN 0 233 98659 6 paperback

Typeset by AKM Associates (UK) Ltd
Ajmal House, Hayes Road, Southall

Printed in Great Britain by
WBC, Bridgend.

CONTENTS

1) Visions of the Bone Idol

2) Ones from the Guardian

3) **Alice looking through the glasses**

4) **Other ones**

M — meaningful
Y — yes my glasses are meaningful

G — grip my head at the sides
L — love is strong so are my glasses
A — attached to my head at the sides
S — stop me walking into opticians
S — see through
E — ever so clean
S — seven quid

Lying about your eyesight

I don't like contact lenses
and can you wonder why
if you want to put one in
you have to poke yourself in the eye
and then they make you cry
especially when they get around the back of your eyeball
they're blinking horriball
don't give them any space
in your face
face up to your glasses

In the arms of my glasses

I go with you across the bridge
foot-sure in your thin embrace
now I am good looking

Poem about my glasses

I look after my spectacles
because they look after me
without my spectacles
where would I be
I'd probably be standing here
but I'd have a job to see
properly

Vision

I have a notion of a nation
where greener grass is
where everyone is trying on everybody else's glasses
where nobody cares about the colour of your skin
or the colour of the case that your glasses are kept in

Black belt

out on the mat the
judo instructor
looks noble in his glasses

Max

(likes to be with people but people don't like to be with Max)

Max is a dog with a problem
the sort of problem it's a job to ignore
the first time they all thought it was funny
but not any more
picture the scene this home loving hound
is sleeping by the fire with the family round
he wakes up and makes a little sound
little Albert gets it first
he's nearest to the ground
Albert's Mum gets wind of it
and she says open the door
and whatever we've been feeding him
I don't think we should give him no more
Max does another one like old kippers
wakes up Daddy in his fireside slippers
Daddy wakes up and says open the door
Albert says it's open Dad I did it when he did it before
then Mum says it's hard to relax with Max about
yesterday it happened while we were out in the car
and it's a small car
and Granny she was sick
she's not used to it like we are
maybe we should swap him for a budgerigar
Max is smelly
he can spoil your telly
but luckily
he's not an elephant

Uncle and auntie

my auntie gives me a colouring book and crayons
I begin to colour
after a while auntie leans over and says
you've gone over the lines
what do you think they're there for
eh?
some kind of statement is it?
going to be a rebel are we?
your auntie gives you a lovely present
and you have to go and ruin it
I begin to cry
my uncle gives me a hanky and some blank paper
do some doggies of your own he says
I begin to colour
when I have done
he looks over
and says they are all very good
he is lying
only some of them are

Bad dog

the dog got my glasses the other day
I thought I'd have to chuck them away
but luckily they were alright

Poem about losing my glasses

the place is unfamiliar
my face is bare
I've mislaid my glasses
I've looked in my glasses case
but they're not there
and I need my glasses
to find my glasses
but I'll be alright
I've got a spare pair

somewhere

Rowena

I was keener on Rowena
than I'd ever been on anyone before
and one night she came round
she said she wanted some excitement
then she pulled me to the ground
I took off my glasses
turned the telly down
and started getting down to business
after I'd done the business
I felt FANTASTIC
like I'd melted in a flame
but Rowena never felt the same
she said she had more excitement
when her last gas bill came
then she kicked my glasses across the room
damaged one of the little windows
and twisted the frame
up
oh Rowena oh woe woe Rowena
she said I was dead below the belt
and above the belt
and as I felt around for my glasses
you don't know how I felt
(around for my glasses)
she said I had done the business
like I was the only one there
she said I was totally unaware
of what she wanted and that all I wanted
was someone who just wanted to lie there
I said look what you've done to my glasses
they are in need of repair
but did Rowena care about my distress
the answer is not yes
she said those glasses suit you now
John

they are a mess
she said you get up my nose
and its time I had a pick
she said she'd had more fun in bed
with a dead matchstick
I said when were you in bed
with a dead matchstick Rowena?
jealousy's a terrible thing
and she said hold your breath for ever
that should do the trick
you're even thicker than your glasses
less of that Rowena I commanded
don't you ever talk about my glasses like that again
ALRIGHT I said
but she'd already gone
I never saw her go though[1]

[1] I never had my glasses on

Hard to handle

you ask me how I'm feeling
I'm afraid I must confide
I'm not exactly full of beans
I've just seen a suicide
and I could have stopped it
but I was far too slow
and the one who copped it I know
or rather knew
only too well
I'm feeling pretty low
my dog just jumped from a seventh floor window

Very bad dog

I took Rover over to the park the other day
I met another bloke with another dog on the way
his dog was an alsatian
my dog was not
he said is that dog an alsatian
I said no
and he said why don't you get a proper dog?
and I said Rover
ignore this copper
and I pick up a stick
and I hold it over Rover
and say Rover
jump out of the clover
and get stuck into the stick
and Rover jumps out of the clover
and bites me in the arm
ALARM ALARM
my dog my dog why hast thou mistaken me?
I am not calm
my dog has done me harm
in my arm
I show him the toothmarks
see Rover where the skin is mauver
Rover sees these nasty marks
he barks
and he begs
for forgiveness
yet I know I must break his legs

Lament of a glasses case

you go out to do a full day's work
I remain shut up and empty
my job is looking after you
I do it very well
and yet you never return with open arms

The death of a scoutmaster

how I remember the old scoutmaster
nobody could start a camp-fire faster
I can see the old scoutmaster in the old scout hut
saying always carry a plaster
in case you cut yourself
if it doesn't happen to you it could happen to your dog
you could be chopping up the firewood
when you mistake him for a log
if it doesn't happen to your dog
it could happen to your glasses
they could be knocked to the floor
by the long arm of the law
when you're standing on the corner
and a copper on a push-bike signalling a left turn passes by
if it's friend you need you need a friend indeed
you need a plaster
you need your money and your keys
but more than these you need a plaster
always carry a plaster our scoutmaster told us
they found one in his pocket
the day a bus ran over him

My mum's dog

Yorkie won't go for a walkie
the only order he'll obey is stay
the only trick he does is sit
he's a rip off

Yorkie in his Mobile Kennel

My brother's joke shop

my brother runs a joke shop
the joke stops there
a family enters
mother
father
and small daughter
Dad's eye is caught by the "giant glasses"
they're a size he says pointing
his daughter tries them on
are they funny she asks her father and mother
they are three-ninety says my brother

My brother's glasses

my brother's glasses
are very different from mine
and one day I said to my brother
Hey! let's try on each other's glasses
and do you know what he said[2]
that's right he said no

[2] here the reader says 'no'

Grandad's glasses

we never used to ask questions
about his glasses
he needed them to see the telly
and that was that
but then one day
he couldn't see the telly anymore
so he didn't need his glasses
What were we to do?
it seemed wrong to throw away the glasses
and there was no point in burying them with him
because
a) his eyes were shut
and b) none of us believed in telly after death
we had a family get together about it
and after the big argument
we came up with two possibilities
a) find someone with glasses like grandad's
and give them the glasses
and b) find someone with glasses like grandad's
and sell them the glasses

Grandma's glasses

my grandmother used to say
before you moan
about the muck on someone else's glasses
make sure you're not on about the muck on your own

her glasses were filthy

The jumble sale

the doors open
everyone comes in
pushing
grabbing
looking
for bargains
a dog comes in too
but nobody notices him
everyone is too busy
looking
for bargains
the man who collects the going-in money
says there are many bargains
everyone is glad
Mr. Hammond sees some gloves
and says these gloves will come in handy
Mrs. Hill buys a jug
Mr. Hill buys a mug
Mr. Lewis buys a plug
Mrs. Lewis buys a mug
and Mr Hammond buys a sleeveless pullover
and puts it on
the dog
wags its tail
he is enjoying the jumble sale too
Mr. Hammond says don't worry anyone
my sleeveless pullover is 'armless
everybody laughs
it is all good fun at the jumble sale
someone treads on the dog
but soon he is alright again

God is dog

in the beginning was the dog
the real name of Jehovah is Rover
Adam's rib is buried in the garden

The death of a dog

the dog died the other day[3]
I buried her where she had buried her bones
and on the levelled earth
laid out her name in stones
about to pick a rose to stick in her grave
action froze
a thorn had torn my thumb
I saw the blood come
and the knowledge that I too
would one day be dead
struck me like a shovel in the features
I fell into an appalling gloom
the bloom remained unpicked
you're going to die I mumbled
as I replaced the shovel in the toolshed
you're going to die
said the sky
as I went up the path
back in the kitchen
I was massively oppressed
by the prospect of the end
but as I looked at the bright yellow bowl
from which my friend had fed
and the length of lead by which she
and sometimes I had been led
from somewhere
I somehow drew strength
I remembered a book I'd read that said
if you lived for ever
you need never try to do anything
as you would do everything
an infinite number of times anyway
so the fact that we are going to die

[3] she choked on my glasses

33

I reasoned
is our reason for living
so come on Johnny boy
live boy live I shouted
I slammed my foot into the dog food bowl
and sent it scudding through imaginary goal posts
you're going to die
so yippie aye aye I whooped
as I dragged an unopened box
of little dog biscuits out of the cupboard
and tore into it oblivious to the coupon
you're going to die
I trumpeted like an elephant
and I tossed those dry nutritious
fawn coloured fragments
that my dog could never know
into the air
like so many pieces of confetti
you're going to die
I roared like the yeti
and I began barking exactly like "Hunter" used to
then I grabbed hold of her big rubber bone
whacked it on the draining board a few times
and hurled it upwards with such force
that it made a mark on the ceiling
you're going to die
I bellowed
you're going to die
I screamed
YOU'RE GOING TO DIE
the door bell rang
it was the bloke from upstairs
he said
I'll kill you if you don't shut up

Bonfire Night

the doors open
everyone comes out
everyone is ready
for fireworks
except the dog
Eddie
he is shut up in the sheddie
even out of doors they have indoor fireworks
Dad says it is better to be safe than dead
the air is full of the smell of next door's fireworks
Mum says they are very good this year
this year Christopher is allowed
to help his dad to light the fireworks
he is very excited
he is very proud
he is twenty-eight

2) Ones from the Guardian

For an old wizard

your boy brought me to you
in the hot Welsh hills
I had lost a love
and thought I'd not recover
soon after my arrival
you dished me up a plate
heaped to stupidity
with mashed potato
and all I thought of
was her
the next morning
you got us up at eight
(you'd let us lie in 'til late)
and you made us spade out potatoes
until that baking day's close
until all I thought of
was potatoes

For his boy

your old man's gone Andrew
without his glasses
and without his stick
you got on his wick
and you were the light of it

Mr Brezhnev

Mr Brezhnev is dead
he may have been a red
but something that he wasn't
was a red under the bed
he was too well fed

Unfortunates

jack-in-the-boxes without springs
jackdaws without wings
lumberjacks with broken backs
and both their arms in slings
these are a few of my favourite images

Poem from the gallows

It never said anything about this
in my horrorscope,
nope:
rope slung
floor dropped
tongue tied
eyes popped,
I am to be a pendulum
marking out moments no longer mine.
They're letting loose
their gruesome noose
and I am going to have a very sore throat indeed

A weekend diary

FRIDAY
Hot.
Stretched out on hilltop all afternoon
wondering am I in wrong job?
Bloody Judas.

SATURDAY
Stayed in.

SUNDAY
Woke up feeling brilliant.
Visited friends – surprised to see me.

Blackburn and Preston

one of the main differences
between Blackburn and Preston
is that Preston
is more western

Photo in St James' Park

a hot spring day by the lake
and a young woman and man
probably tourists
possibly Spanish
who wanted a photo of themselves together
handed their camera to someone
almost definitely English
who certain fellow countrymen
might   predictably describe
as a very drunken old dosser
but to them he was just a passer by
he accepted the camera
took a long time focusing
and steadying himself
but managed to take the picture
and received genuine gratitude
from the two
who had seen nothing deviant in his behaviour
and who would remember him
as a friendly and helpful
English gentleman
if he hadn't fallen into the lake
with their camera

Lent

Lent is meant
to be spent fasting
in remembrance
of the Lord lasting
six weeks without a decent meal
six weeks in the desert
without any dinner
without any dessert
and without any tent
but he saved on rent
and before he went
he ate plenty of pancakes

York

I went round the Railway Museum
in York
there were plenty of trains
but it was quicker to walk

Bradford to Bristol

from Bradford Yorkshire
to Bristol Temple Meads
you don't have to change your underwear
but you have to change at Leeds

April fools

in France they say
poissons d'Avril
in England
they don't
a good moment to pick
for an April Fools' day trick
is when it is unexpected
like early October

Not waving

I was on a TV magazine show
we'd just discussed
blowing the dust off poetry
and the life of poetry
beyond the grave
and I could see a monitor
with us silhouetted on it a
blackcloth to the credits
and craving a bit of fun
and feeling I'd been unnecessarily grave myself
I waved to camera two
and the floor manager said
we'll do that once more
but without the waving
thank you

Innocent

we were as thin
as a pin
in knowledge
at the college of each other
like two new strips of plasticine
our colours were separate and clean
but we were unlucky
we got all mixed up
and mucky

Guilty

you are guilty
we have your dignity
you are guilty
because examples are needed
you are guilty
because guilt sells better than innocence
and you are guilty
because you stole fifty thousand quid

Untitled

it's hard to make a conscience out of custard
it's hard to hear things when they're very faint
things look cleaner when they've just been dusted
unless it's done with absolute restraint
a missing person's rarely called Xavier
public houses have no patron saint
you'd think they would have canonised the saviour
he'll be coming back and lodging a complaint
if you're somebody who tends to go and burgle
middle class you generally ain't
it's hard to keep your gob shut when you gurgle
especially when you're gurgling with paint
the best words don't sound much with bad diction
the pave meant very little to the kerb
a phone bill without figures is a fiction
a gerbil without illness is a gerb

Beyond comparison

I was scared of you sharing too much with others
you were scared of sharing so much with me
I wanted you most when you were someone else's
you wanted me most when I was my own
your clumsy lies came out of care not cowardice
and although I never lied
I was untrue to what we promised it would never become
but that's only YOUR opinion

Art gallery poem

Cornerhouse—Manchester
and the Whitechapel—Whitechapel
are great
but the apple of them all
the one I really rate
is the Tate
it feels like a mate
I can't wait
for my next re-acquainting
with the place and the painting
I even love the gate
yes the Tate is my Pimlico friend
and I wish it was open
'til ever so late
but I don't know how I'd appreciate it
if I worked there as an attendant

This could be heaven

He's known you for under a week
and he wonders if he's under a spell
it's as if he's been living in a shell
and for the first time ever
he's poked his rocker out.
He feels like a knocker
that's discovered its bell
like some sellotape
realising it's more self-expressive
sticking something
than being stuck on a roll
he feels whole
and it's hell
is it just his imagination
or is it yours as well?

A young artist

twenty seven months or so
you've been sizing up the planet
and looking at this early work
leant on the radiator to dry
I can't say it looks like anything
but maybe you want it to
or perhaps when you began it
you had meant it to
so I ask you
is it a house?
'no'
is it a mouse?
'no'
is it a tortoise?
'no'
well if it's not any of those
what CAN it be?
and you inform me
that it is paint

No new beret

shopping for a new beret
the biggest they had was a 7
but I take a 7½
later on stopping in a café
I realise something in my hair
that shouldn't be there
it is the little size 7 sticker
left over from trying on the beret

Why I didn't get you a valentine's card

because I'm into saving trees
because my declarations are not
    determined by the calendar
because ultimately my heart is my
    own
because I forgot.

On bonfire night

seeing a wigwam of planks
being burned
and concerned
about its future
the nearby fence
looks tense

On the Roman way

true the Roman chariots were slower
but their roads were straighter

in this car
there are no Roman numerals on the clocks
and the doors are outnumbered by locks
I bet the Romans weren't this security conscious
Pontius

The family and the priest

Father Coombes lived next door to Dunbars
and they decided to join forces
to save the world's resources
they had two brooms and two cars between them
and calculated that this exceeded their needs
by one car and one broom
it wasn't difficult to reach an agreement
about a sharing arrangement
and they each got about seventeen hundred quid
for the car they sold
but discovered that an old broom is far more difficult
to get rid of
especially at a car dealers

Winter

piled up on pavement
the white droppings of the sky
and my Dad
swinging his shovel
swishing his broom
lifting the snow
shifting the snow
making sure he doesn't do
any of the next door neighbours' bit

Cork

it floats
and goes in bottles
like somebody buoyant
who can't be bothered
to go to the toilet

Piece of chalk

leaving a legible trail
a long hard snail
without any house

Chalk and cheese

as different as chalk and cheese they say
but there's plenty of things
that are a lot more different than these
a blade of grass
and a pair of glass dungarees
for instance

Poem about not using tropical hardwoods because it diminishes the rain forests

this winter
I hope you get a splinter
if you make a toboggan
and it is a mahog'un

Wipe wipe wipe your glasses

I've seen people with mud on their glasses,
I've seen people with blood on their glasses,
Once I saw a lad who had
the leg of a daddy longlegs on his glasses.
He thought they were cracked.
But they weren't.

Jane and Wojtek

Wojtek was a Polish boy in my class when I was about seven, Jane wasn't. I fancied Jane, Jane fancied Wojtek:

when I saw Jane and Wojtek kiss
I was jealous of their bliss
and I reported them to miss

Smelly

one playtime
staying in out of the rain
his heart sank
someone sniffed his seat
and said it stank
a ritual followed
in which you had to dare
to whiff the niffy chair
recoiling from the soiling
in jubilant despair
from that day on we called him Smelly
but one day Smelly wasn't there
gone for good and no one knew where
but you could still smell smelly
if you smelt his chair

Exercise

exercise—your body needs it
exercise is yours for free
exercise your right to protest
exercise your doggie
whatever the colour
whatever the breed
a dog needs exercise
like it needs dogfeed

3) Alice looking through the glasses

Chapter one

Alice why do you call your teddy Furry said Daddy
when he hasn't got any fur?
he does look furry if you stand back a bit said Alice
hmm said Daddy thoughtfully
as he stroked the fur of their sleepy old doggie
(who was called Loggie)
and does anything else look furry if you stand back a bit?
oh yes replied Alice—my bike
my friend Mike—all my friends in fact
in fact—everything
I think it may be things looking BLURRY
not furry said Daddy
but Loggie looks furry and Loggie IS furry protested Alice
yes replied her Dad
but I don't think Mike is
and I'm not sure about your bike either
and he asked if she could see the blackboard in her class at
    school
and Alice said that she could but she couldn't see the writing
I think you need glasses said Daddy

Chapter two

Alice had a fantastic time in the eye test
as she sat in the important looking chair
and when her eyes were being looked at
through the tiny thin torch with the thin tiny glare
she wanted to say that it was rude to stare—just for a joke
but the nice optician might have thought
Alice was being rude herself
so she didn't
she just got on with her eye test in a sensible fashion
and when it was all over the optician put on the big light
and said Alice you have what we opticians call an
   astigmatism
and Alice asked if that meant she could have some glasses
and the optician said she could
and at a very reasonable price too
Alice was very happy
she had passed the examination
and the optician measured Alice's head
and said she would send her a postcard
as soon as the glasses were ready
just wait 'til I tell Teddy
said Alice

Chapter three

while she was looking forward to her new spectacles
a vile boy in Alice's class
told her that she would be a silly old four eyes if she wore
   glasses
Alice replied that he was the silly one
because glasses weren't eyes they were glasses
she was not going to let HIM bully her
into wearing contact lenses!
the next day Alice's postcard came
she was sad that her surname had been spelt wrongly
but she was very glad
as she left home with her Dad
because she knew that when she returned
she would be clad in her glasses
and when they arrived back in Glassesland
all the brightly coloured frames on display
made Alice even more excited
and the receptionist
searched through her big boxful of glasses cases
for Alice's prescription
they don't appear to be here dear
she mumbled
as she rummaged
and the happiness went out of Alice
like air from a broken balloon
she had been too happy too soon
they're not there cried Alice THEY'RE NOT THERE
but it turned out that they were there
it was just that her surname had been mis-spelt on the label
and soon lying on the table
was a beautiful snappy red glasses case
and Alice was being placed into the arms of her brand new
   glasses
and something incredible occurred
nothing looked blurred any more!
just wait 'til I see Teddy said Alice
in the crystal palace of her glasses

Chapter four

ooh they're fantastic said Alice
what do you think Daddy?
I think those glasses are spectacular said Daddy
making a little joke
and the receptionist started laughing
and Alice started laughing as well
not because she understood the joke
but because she was so happy with her glasses
then suddenly all the laughing stopped
the snappy red glasses case lying on the table
started snapping open and shut
and as it did so a little voice came out saying
although those glasses look fantastic
they're not glass they're sort of plastic
oh shut up you cheeky chappie said Alice
to snappy the talking glasses case
we were having a jolly good laugh until you butted in
and when the glasses case had shut up
Alice thought that maybe she had been rather rude
but then she told herself that you can't really be rude
to a glasses case
and she went over to look at her new glasses in the mirror
oh do look Daddy she said
there's a little crack in the mirror
and Daddy came over and looked at the mirror
then looked at Alice's glasses
and said that's no crack in the mirror Alice
that's the leg of a Daddy Long Legs on your glasses
and that's where your glasses cloth comes in
(Daddy knew because Daddy wore glasses too)
and Alice opened her glasses case
and was just about to remove
the little oblong of cleaning material

(the glasses cloth)
when Snappy (the talking glasses case)
started screaming and screaming
what's wrong now snapped Alice
please don't remove my tongue pleaded Snappy
that glasses cloth is my tongue!
Alice looked a bit shocked
but then Snappy said that he was only joking
and they had a jolly good laugh
she had understood Snappy's joke
and hoped that when she got home
Teddy wouldn't be jealous or angry with her
for finding a new friend

Chapter five

on the way home Alice was amazed
as she gazed at the world through her new glasses
she could read so much more from a distance
the store signs and street signs and the places to eat signs
and you didn't have to wait until the bus got to the bus stop
before you could tell what number it was
mind you—you still got disappointed
when you found out that it was the wrong one
but you couldn't blame your glasses for that could you!
when they got to the door of their house
Loggie the doggie never barked
he NEVER barked
he was always asleep

that's why he was called Loggie
Alice went straight upstairs to show her specs to Teddy
there he was all tucked up in bed
only he looked different
much less blurry
what do you think of the glasses then?
said Alice proudly showing them off
Teddy seemed to like them
and Alice started making him
a small pair of brown paper glasses of his own
like she'd seen them do on Blue Peter
and she told him that if he wanted a home for them
he could share her glasses case
that's me said Snappy *I'm Alice's new friend*
and Teddy didn't get angry or jealous at all
because he thought it was very healthy
for Alice to have a number of friends
and anyway he could share Snappy too
and so Alice and Teddy
went happily to sleep in their new glasses
all the better to see in their dreams
but I'm afraid this was rather silly
and in the morning Alice's father hurried into her bedroom
because he heard screaming
and it wasn't Snappy this time and it wasn't a joke
it had even woken up Loggie and given him a nasty fright
Teddy's glasses were alright
but Alice's were all broken
from where they had fallen off
and been rolled on in the night!
so remember if you're not a Ted
don't wear your glasses on your head in bed
put them in your glasses case instead

P.S. luckily Alice's Dad had secretly got her a spare pair
and the story ended
with Alice looking splendid

4) Other ones

Living in a mobile home

my Mum lives in a mobile home
it may sound odd to some
but does it to my Mum?
no—it doesn't to my Mum
it may be small but she's not very tall
and she's got all she needs
heating
lighting
hot water
a roof
to tell you the truth when you're inside
it's hard to believe that you're living in a mobile home
she wants to keep her mobile home as long as she can
she doesn't want a mansion or a caravan
a mobile home is just the place for my Mummy
mention a mobile home
and she puts up her thumby
but there's always room for home improvements
even in an ideal home
and whenever there's a windy day
I hope my mother's mobile home won't blow away
because if it did I don't know what my Mum would say
but anyway
there's sliding doors
there's wall to wall floors
and there's plenty of room
so you can have a party
you can let yourself go
you can show a home movie
you can have a game of cricket
with your telly as the wicket
and you can do the bosanova
without knocking your dog over

itsma sweet mobile home

Bit of crumpet

my mother called my brother's first girlfriend crumpet
because once she sent him a postcard from the seaside
depicting a man making a double entendre
about eating a crumpet
and enjoying someone's privates
my brother protested that it was just a bit of fun
and my Mum told him that if the girl was decent
he would bring her to the home
so one day he brought her round for tea
and my Mum asked if she went to the opera
because to her way of thinking
even though she'd never been herself
this was something refined
and when the girl said no
my Mum said never mind dear
you enjoy your crumpet

Pat and the wizard

everything seemed flat to Pat
so she sat on her bike
and cycled round to her uncle Matt the wizard
even though her tyres were flat
and there was a blizzard
so what's the matter Pat said Matt
and Pat explained and Matt said Pat
let me look inside my hat
there's nothing there he looked and said
then put his hat back on his head
and went all red and rolled about
and spat a pair of glasses out
now look through these the wizard said
and Pat she put them on her head
and said
the world's NOT flat
Christopher Columbat
just wait until I tell my cat
she didn't know her cat was dead
splatted flat by uncle Fred
it's lucky uncle Matt was skilled
at mending cats his brother killed
and that's exactly what he did
and all he charged was fifty pence

A depressing incident

This is about people getting their bit at the expense of everyone else. The background is the intensification of privatisation and personal isolation: the reflector spectacles which make the eyes of the wearer inscrutable, the one-person-operated buses where drivers are too busy to communicate, the no-person-operated cash points and the prevalence of video—a significant move to private consumption away from the shared experience of networked television, with video libraries now outnumbering public libraries. The depletion of public libraries and public corporations takes THE WORD public out of circulation and subsequently diminishes the significance of THE IDEA. That's the background, this is the poem:

once when I was sat on the tube
this bloke sat next to me
and pushed my elbow off the armrest

Sport

sport sport there is many a sort
of sport
pole vault
long and short distance running
horse racing
noughts and crosses
is not one
sport is good for the body sport is good for the soul
sport is thought-provoking
sport is wholesome
wholesome sports equipment in your hands
and you'll see what I'm on about
sport is a port in a storm
if you are depressed
some sport ought to sort you out pretty sharpish
remember in this crazy world
sport is NORMAL
sport—I'll spell it out for you
S – stimulating
P – popular
O – oxygenating
R – really intersting
T – a nice cup of tea goes down a treat after a bit of sport
but the other day I met someone who did not like sport!
they did not like sport because they thought
it was all about winning
so I told 'em
of course it's not all about winning
someone's got to lose
AIN'T YA!

Dreaming my Dad

in my hospital dream
the doctor is glad I have come
the sister is relieved
there isn't long and they haven't told him
I enter the ward
the heads poke out of holes in the centre of the beds
like the heads of swimmers poking through the sea
I think this is ridiculous
but remember it is a dream
down the identity parade of the sick
I seek out the face that is familiar
he is easily spotted
unlike the others all of him is visible
boy-like without bedclothes curled in stripey pyjamas
I sit up on his borrowed bed
and think to think I nearly came tomorrow
the tears begin
I try to hold them in
I do not want him to know the doctor's terrible omission
I know how he likes that doctor
I cry more now
now surely he must realise
and I must open my squeezed-up eyes
and share his knowledge –
before my Dad has died
we must both be crucified
and quietly he turns away from me
saying he wants to sleep
and for a moment of dream confusion
I feel another pain
here is a lover rejecting my desire
and then he is my Dad again
doing the unbelievable
the biggest one of all
he is letting me off
you've suffered enough son he says
have a toffee

The sleeping train spotter

dreaming old smokers
with stokers to feed 'em
he noted the numbers
but couldn't quite read 'em

Looking after your dog

there's a man whose doggie bit the boy next door
because he pushed her owner to the floor
and the bitten boy's bite looked rather bad
and the father showed the law his lad
and the law told the owner that things looked grim
and he told his doggie what the law told him
and the dog jumped up and said hello
she had no idea she had to go
she didn't know
it was death row
for doggie
and the owner knew it was time to act
the boy deserved to be attacked
he picked her up and made a pact
and he bought a gun from a criminal contact
I can see the owner's point of view
you've got to look out for them that look out for you

dog and owner settle down
behind a barricade
the owner's rearranged the flat
and taken up the welcome mat his sister made
and a doggie barks at a marksman
on the roof across the street
a different doggie from the one whose life
they've come here to complete
the Labrador the law must turn into a slab of meat

the megaphone is calling for a sensible end
but a man's got to stand by a man's best friend
the home's become a castle
the thing's become a siege
and the dog looks up as if to say
I want to go for a walkies my liege
and the doggie in the basket hears her king
say I think they're coming I can hear something
now where did I put that blessed gun?
I can never remember what I've done with things
oh you're lying on it!
and he pulls the gun with a sudden jerk
and the trigger gets caught in the wickerwork
so the gun goes off
and the dog will soon
and the marksman stiffens
in the afternoon sun
and a bullet breaks the window and the owner's skin
he couldn't see the marksman looking in
and then they break the door in
and the owner lets them have it
a piece of his mind
he says what kind of government
lets a programme like Blue Peter
organise the guide dogs for the blind?

What have you got to do?

you haven't GOT to go to the bank
and you haven't GOT to go to the toilet
you CHOOSE to
I suppose you have got to look after the children
but only because you chose to have them to begin with
we say we've got to do things
to make our existence seem necessary
which of course it isn't
there are only two things you've GOT to do
live
and buy my poetry books

Anger

A classroom.
Sound of noisy pre-class disruption.
Enter teacher, he walks to his desk and stands waiting
for silence, a paper aeroplane hits him in the glasses
Noise stops abruptly.
Pause—teacher quietly seething.
He turns to blackboard and writes A-N-G-E-R.
He turns back to the class,
and without emotion, begins the lesson:
A – An extreme form of annoyance.
N – 'Nobody talks to me like that,' is a fairly common phrase
   used in association with this emotion.
G – 'Go and comb your hair John, if you leave this house
   without combing your hair I'll come down your school and
   comb it for you in front of all your friends if you've got
   any,' is not so common.
E – Emptying a bucket of latrine slops into someone's sleeping
   bag can cause an angry reaction especially if the person is
   still in it.
R – Rage is an extreme form of anger and so is wrath but
   wrath doesn't begin with an 'r'.
He is more cheerful now.
Sound of Elvis Costello's 'I'm not angry'. Teacher dances.
Dancing and music stop.
Immense disruption—teacher peppered with paper
   aeroplanes.

He's in love with a brown paper bag

his mother she was disappointed
it's not exactly what she had in mind
but eventually she came to accept it
how could a mother reject it
he's in love and love isn't easy to find
people stop and people stare
people say they're a crazy pair
but there's many a crazy scene
between a husband and a wife
he found it by a market stall
it's a bit screwed up but aren't we all
an empty bag is better than an empty life
and he doesn't mind if you caress
his little scrap of happiness
he's in love but he doesn't want to possess
and one day he came up to me
he held the bag so tenderly
and he held it out to me
and I said thanks a lot
but I don't think I could cope
I've already got a steady relationship
with a light blue envelope
it was nice of you to offer though

I feel like a suitcase

they fill me up with just about
as much as I can take
then they put some more in
and they wonder why I break
and they stick labels on me

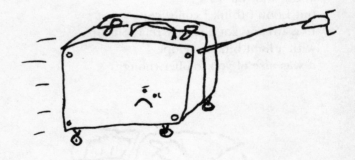

Electrical

You provide the vital spark
you are electrical like a copper's torch in the dark.
We may be poles apart
but that's the attraction
negative and positive
heart to heart.
You're hard to resist
and my resistance is low
you're irresistible
you are electrical
and you'll be missed when you go.

Betrayal

Somehow you look different tonight,
there's something there
that wasn't there before.
There's a glint in your eyes
I'm not exactly sure what it is
I can't quite put my finger on it,
then I realise:
contact lenses.

Love poem by my dog

I saw you in the park
I wanted to be your friend
I tunnelled my snout
up your non-barking end